Gal Gadot

Gal Gadot

SOLDIER, MODEL, WONDER WOMAN

JILL SHERMAN

LERNER PUBLICATIONS ◆ MINNEAPOLIS

Lerner Publications Company
A division of Lerner Publishing Group, Inc.
241 First Avenue North
Minneapolis, MN USA 55401

For reading levels and more information, look up this title at www.lernerbooks.com.

The images in this book are used with the permission of: Kathy Hutchins/Shutterstock.com, p. 2; Dia Dipasupil/Getty Images, p. 6; Christophel/Alamy Stock Photo, pp. 8, 34, 37, 38, 39; Mike Coppola/Getty Images, pp. 9, 10; Moviestore Collection Ltd/Alamy Stock Photo, pp. 11, 22; PS-I/Alamy Stock Photo, p. 12; Jane Sweeney/Getty Images, p. 13; Amos Ben Gershom, p. 15; Martin Bernetti/AFP/Getty Images, p. 16; Pavel Wolberg/Moment/Getty Images, p. 17; Corinna Kern/NurPhoto/Getty Images, p. 18; Jack Guez/AFP/Getty Images, p. 19; Dave J Hogan/Getty Images, p. 20; Entertainment Pictures/Alamy Stock Photo, pp. 23, 35; Boris Horvat/AFP/Getty Images, p. 24; Photo 12/Alamy Stock Photo, pp. 25, 26, 28, 30, 31; Jason Merritt/Getty Images, p. 27; Michael Tran/FilmMagic/Getty Images, p. 32; DC ENTERTAINMENT/WARNER BROS./Newscom, p. 36.

Front cover: Gregg DeGuire/WireImage/Getty Images.

Main body text set in Rotis Serif Std 55 Regular 13.5/17. Typeface provided by Adobe Systems.

Library of Congress Cataloging-in-Publication Data

Names: Sherman, Jill, author.
Title: Gal Gadot : soldier, model, wonder woman / Jill Sherman.
Description: Minneapolis : Lerner Publications, [2018] | Series: Gateway Biographies | Ages 9–14, Grades 4–6. | Includes bibliographical references and index.
Identifiers: LCCN 2017041218 (print) | LCCN 2017042135 (ebook) | ISBN 9781541523593 (eb pdf) | ISBN 9781541523586 (lb : alk. paper) | ISBN 9781541543706 (pb : alk. paper)
Subjects: LCSH: Gadot, Gal, 1985– | Jewish women—Israel—Biography—Juvenile literature. | Actresses—Israel—Biography—Juvenile literature.
Classification: LCC CT1919.P38 (print) | LCC CT1919.P38 S3156 2018 (ebook) | DDC 792.02/8092 [B] —dc23

LC record available at https://lccn.loc.gov/2017041218

Manufactured in the United States of America
1-45146-35947-11/30/2017

Contents

Gal Gadot in New York City in October 2017.

Photographers and reporters gathered around the blue carpet outside the Hollywood Pantages Theatre in Hollywood, California, on May 25, 2017. Nearby, men and women dressed in costumes and T-shirts emblazoned with a yellow W logo crowded into bleachers and lined up behind metal barricades. Excitement hung in the air as the crowd grew. They were there for the world premiere of the movie *Wonder Woman.* Soon many of the stars of the film would arrive, including Gal Gadot (pronounced *gall guh-dote*), the actor who played Wonder Woman.

Gadot arrived in a glittery red gown and flat gold sandals. She smiled and waved to the crowd as she walked quickly down the carpet. She talked with fans and signed pictures and posters. Photographers and reporters took photos and asked questions. They wanted to know why she wasn't wearing heels—she said her flat sandals were more comfortable—and they asked her about the movie and what it was like to play Wonder Woman.

Gadot performs as Wonder Woman in a scene from the 2017 movie.

Wonder Woman tells the story of Diana Prince, an immortal Amazonian princess. When a World War I (1914–1918) pilot crashes near her home island, Diana rescues him. Then the pair leave the island to end the war and save the world from destruction. "I think it's so important that we have . . . strong female figures to look up to, and Wonder Woman is an amazing one," Gadot said. "It's great that . . . finally she gets her own movie."

Soon another star appeared on the carpet. She hugged Gadot, and the two began posing for photos together. It was Lynda Carter, the actor who played Wonder Woman in a 1970s TV series. Gadot and Carter were thrilled to be able to celebrate Wonder Woman together. Carter was excited that Wonder Woman could inspire young girls again. She later said that *Wonder Woman* was a great movie and that Gadot had done a great job in the role.

Many people think superhero movies are something only boys enjoy. Batman, Spider-Man, and Iron Man dominate theaters, and boys and men fill the seats; girls and women watch superhero movies too. Movies about female superheroes, such as the 2004 *Catwoman*, starring Halle Berry, have not done very well with fans and critics. But some people in Hollywood thought it was time for a woman to take the lead in another major superhero film.

Actors Gal Gadot (L) and Jason Momoa greet fans during the 'Justice League' autograph signing at Comic-Con International 2017 at San Diego Convention Center on July 22, 2017 in San Diego, California.

The movie's director, Patty Jenkins, said, "I think the world needs all types of superheroes."

Not everyone agreed. Critics wondered whether this female-led superhero film would be successful. They feared that audiences would respond as they had to *Catwoman*. But *Wonder Woman* was a hit. The company that made the movie thought the film would earn about $65 million in the United States. But *Wonder Woman* far exceeded expectations. During its opening weekend in the United States, the movie made $103 million. One month after its release, the film had made more than $700 million worldwide. Gadot's portrayal of Wonder Woman was a huge success. Film critics and filmmakers took note. And fans look forward to seeing more female superheroes on the big screen.

Origin Story

Comic book writer William Moulton Marston created
Wonder Woman in 1941. Marston was interested in
women's rights and the women's suffrage movement,
when, from 1848 to 1920, many women in the United
States fought for the right to vote. Marston had noticed a
lack of women in comics. He thought there was too much
violence in comic books, and he wanted to emphasize
powers such as love, truth, and beauty. He knew such
stories would be popular with girls and would show them
that they could do anything.

Wonder Woman's story was rebooted and revamped a
number of times over the years. Though the details and
costumes changed, Wonder Woman remained a strong
role model. In 1974 a television movie based on Wonder
Woman aired. The next year, a television series was
released, starring Lynda Carter as Wonder Woman. The
show aired for three seasons until 1979.

Childhood in Israel

Gal was born in Rosh HaAyin, Israel, on April 30, 1985. She grew up there with her parents, Irit and Michael Gadot, and her younger sister, Dana. Their father was an engineer. Their mother was a physical education teacher. Gal's parents raised their daughters to be confident and to have ambition. It was a sentiment that Gal took to heart. "I'm not saying that I'm stronger than most men," she later said, "but we all have the same brains and we can achieve the same things."

Rosh HaAyin, Israel

Gal was raised in a traditional Jewish household. She and her family attended temple and celebrated Jewish holidays. Her faith and Israeli identity remained important to her into adulthood. "I want people to have a good impression of Israel. I don't feel like I'm an ambassador for my country, but I do talk about Israel a lot—I enjoy telling people about where I come from and my religion."

Even at a young age, Gal was confident and determined. When she was three years old, her parents threw a party on the rooftop of their house. Her parents had put their young daughter to bed. But when she heard people coming into the house, Gal became upset that she was not included in the festivities. The toddler snuck out of bed and climbed onto the roof. When the adults still didn't notice her, she grabbed a hose and began to spray water on the entire party "just to get attention."

A synagogue, or temple, is a Jewish place of worship. This synagogue is in Jerusalem.

Gal was an active child. She didn't watch much TV. Instead, she played outside. She was full of energy, and she participated in a number of sports. Her mother taught Gal to swim when she was very young, and Gal also played tennis and volleyball. Gal's height gave her an advantage on the basketball court. But she especially liked dancing. For twelve years she practiced ballet, hip-hop, jazz, and modern dance.

As a teenager, Gal worked typical jobs. She began babysitting for her neighbors at the age of twelve. When she was fifteen years old, she got a job at Burger King. But she dreamed of one day becoming a dance choreographer, someone who plans and creates the movements for dancers in a performance.

Model Citizen

Growing up, people occasionally approached Gadot with modeling opportunities. She was never interested in being a model. But in 2004, when Gadot was eighteen years old, a talent scout noticed her. He asked her to enter the Miss Israel beauty pageant. She thought this seemed like the kind of thing that would be fun to tell her grandchildren about one day, so Gadot agreed to enter the pageant.

During the Miss Israel pageant, Gadot participated in a variety of events. She had interviews and wore evening gowns. She and her fellow contestants performed a special song. It was a Hebrew version of singer Irene Cara's hit song from 1980, "Fame." Judges watched each part of the pageant to choose the top contestants.

When it was down to the final contestants, Gadot was surprised to find herself still standing on the stage. But she stood poised and serene, wearing a silvery white dress. The host announced the names of the runners-up. Then it was time to announce the winner. When the host announced that Gadot had won the pageant, she was completely shocked. She was crowned Miss Israel 2004. This meant she would also represent Israel in that year's Miss Universe pageant. Gadot had not expected to win, and she was nervous about the responsibility of representing Israel.

Gadot wears her Miss Israel crown after winning the 2004 pageant.

Gal Gadot, Miss Israel, arrives at the Miss Universe pageant in Quito, Ecuador.

The Miss Universe pageant was held in Ecuador that year. There, Gadot met young women from around the globe. But the eighteen-year-old felt uncomfortable and out of place. Winning Miss Israel had been fun, but she'd had enough of competing in pageants. She had been surprised to win Miss Israel, and she didn't want to win Miss Universe too. So she rebelled.

Gadot showed up late to pre-pageant events. She refused to wear makeup. The contestants were expected to wear gowns to many of the events. But Gadot would show up in her regular clothing, saying, "No way am I having breakfast in a gown!"

It came as no surprise that Gadot was not the pageant winner. Instead, that year's crown went to Jennifer Hawkins of Australia. Gadot went back home to Israel.

At the age of twenty, Gadot began her service in the Israel Defense Forces (IDF). All Israeli citizens are required to serve in the military. Men and women over the age of eighteen enlist in the IDF. Men typically serve three years, and women serve two.

Gadot's service began with a grueling four-month boot camp. During boot camp, soldiers undergo intense physical training. Gadot and the other soldiers went on long runs. They also completed workouts including sit-ups and push-ups. The soldiers learned about the different kinds of weapons they might use in combat. They practiced shooting in all kinds of different positions and situations. Boot camp is intense so soldiers can be ready to fight.

Female soldiers in the IDF undergo training in the Negev desert in Israel.

A group of Israeli soldiers prepares for a training drill.

As a natural athlete, Gadot found the boot camp's physical demands relatively easy to bear. Her assignment after boot camp was as a combat trainer. Gadot taught gymnastics and led workouts. She proudly remembers that "the soldiers loved me because I made them fit."

In 2006 Gadot was serving in the IDF during the Israel-Hezbollah War. That July, Hezbollah, a political party in Lebanon, crossed the Israel border to raid an Israeli military patrol. This marked the start of the war. After just a month of fighting, the United Nations stepped in to stop the conflict.

Gadot did not see combat herself as her role in the IDF was to train soldiers, but she has stood in support of her country and the IDF. Gadot says she wishes no country needed to have a military, but her experience in the IDF taught her about responsibility and hard work. "In Israel serving is part of being an Israeli," she says. "You've got to give back to the state. You give two or three years, and it's not about you. You give your freedom away. You learn discipline and respect."

IDF soldiers complete a military training exercise.

Modeling Career

After her Miss Israel win, Gadot was flooded with modeling opportunities. After she finished her service in the Israeli Defense Forces, she became the face of Israel's Castro clothing line. In 2007 she appeared in *Maxim's* "Women of the Israeli Army" photo shoot. She has also modeled in international campaigns for the fashion brand Miss Sixty and for Huawei smartphones. In 2015 Gadot became the face of Gucci's new fragrance, Bamboo. She says she still enjoys modeling because it is similar to acting. Both are very creative jobs.

Catching the Acting Bug

After completing her military service, Gadot turned her focus to her career. She enrolled in Interdisciplinary Center (IDC) Herzliya, a university in Herzliya, Israel. There, she studied law and international relations. Gadot hoped to become a lawyer.

But she was also still modeling. Soon a casting director approached her with a possible acting role. She asked Gadot to consider auditioning for a role in the upcoming James Bond movie *Quantum of Solace.*

"No way," Gadot responded. She was committed to her studies. Gadot saw herself doing work that she thought was more serious than acting. Besides, Gadot mostly spoke Hebrew, and the script for the movie was in English. Gadot could speak English, but she wasn't entirely comfortable with it. The idea of being in a James Bond movie just seemed too far-fetched.

Even so, the idea grew on her, and she eventually agreed to audition. In the end, the role went to Ukrainian actor Olga Kurylenko instead. But because of the audition, Gadot began to really enjoy acting. She remembers thinking, "This is so much more fun than law school!"

Gadot decided to give acting a try. She let her agent know that she was interested in doing more auditions. She also hired an acting coach to help her develop her skills. A month later, she got her first role as Miriam "Merry" Elkayam in the Israeli television series *Bubot.* The show was about the drama and intrigue of the modeling world.

The Fast and the Furious franchise began in 2001 with its first movie about street racing.

With this success, Gadot made the decision to drop out of law school. She wanted to give acting her all. Just three months after she landed her role on *Bubot*, Gadot got another call. It was the same casting agent who had suggested she audition for the Bond movie. This time, the agent suggested that she audition for a role in *Fast & Furious*, the fourth movie in the successful Fast and the Furious franchise.

Going Hollywood

Gadot sent out her audition tape for the *Fast & Furious* role immediately. Soon she was on a plane on her way to Los Angeles to audition for the part.

The first movie in the series, *The Fast and the Furious*, came out in 2001. It starred actor Vin Diesel as Dominic Toretto, an elite street racer and auto mechanic.

He became involved in illegal street racing and robberies. But despite his criminal enterprises, Toretto had a strong moral code of family and loyalty.

The next two movies—*2 Fast 2 Furious* (2003) and *The Fast and the Furious: Tokyo Drift* (2006)—focused on different aspects of the street-racing world. Diesel was not involved in the second movie and appeared only briefly in the third.

Paul Walker (*left*) and Diesel act in a scene for *Fast & Furious.*

The third movie made less money than the first two, and producers thought the franchise might be becoming less popular with audiences. They considered releasing more movies that would go directly to DVD rather than appearing in theaters. But fans had been thrilled to see Diesel's return in the third movie. It was enough to convince Diesel and the producers to keep the film series going. Diesel agreed to return to play the main character. He also signed on as a producer for the fourth movie. The producers wanted to show less street racing and focus more on action scenes and robberies. They also wanted a diverse cast. Michelle Rodriguez, who had been in the first movie, agreed to return, and actors such as Chris "Ludacris" Bridges and Sung Kang helped round out the large cast.

Since the fourth movie, the Fast and the Furious franchise has continued to work with large and diverse casts. This diversity has helped make the franchise even more popular with fans.

Gadot on the set of *Fast & Furious*

In Hollywood, Gadot met with the casting agents, producers, and the director of the film, Justin Lin. They asked her to read lines with Diesel. She was nervous, but the two worked well together on camera. Gadot went home while they made their final casting choices.

Two weeks later, they called with their decision. She had the part! Gadot would be playing the role of Gisele Yashar. Gadot's background in the Israel Defense Forces helped her land the part. Her knowledge of weapons and combat tactics impressed the director. In a high-action, stunt-filled movie, these talents would certainly come in handy.

One month later, Gadot found herself on the set as part of the Fast and the Furious family. It was her first big Hollywood movie. She was working with stars Vin Diesel, Paul Walker, and Michelle Rodriguez. Gadot loved

Gadot does a *Fast & Furious* scene with (*left to right*) Diesel, Laz Alonso, and John Ortiz.

working with this superstar cast. "We all have such great chemistry," said Gadot. "It really shows on screen, and also it is very rare to see such a big cast in one movie, and everyone who goes to see this movie can relate to at least one of the characters."

Gadot was a great fit for the action flick. Typically, actors in action movies have stunt doubles to perform intense action sequences. Stunt professionals know how to do dangerous stunts without becoming injured. Actors perform safer parts of the stunts if they need to appear on camera. But Gadot has a thrill-seeking streak. Off set, she owns a motorcycle. So she told the director, "I want to be a tough girl. . . . I want to be flying in the air, on a motorcycle. And I want to do it by myself."

The director put her in the driver's seat. Gadot learned to drive a Porsche Cayman like a pro. She performed as many stunts as she was able, but she did have a stunt double for some of the more intense action sequences.

Fast & Furious opened on April 3, 2009. Gadot attended her first Hollywood premiere and walked the red carpet with her castmates. She was nervous, but she remained poised as she posed for photographers.

Audiences flocked to the theaters. The film made more than $70 million in its opening weekend. Although she was unknown to American audiences at the time, Gadot gained attention for her role in the film. Her performance with Diesel drew people in. There was little doubt that this was the beginning of an impressive career in Hollywood.

Gadot poses for a photo at the premiere of *Fast & Furious.*

The Success of the Furious

The Fast and the Furious movies make up one of the most successful movie franchises in history. With the release of the eighth movie, *The Fate of the Furious*, in 2017, the franchise has made more than $5 billion. It is one of the top moneymaking franchises in history, behind big names such as Star Wars, James Bond, Harry Potter, and Lord of the Rings.

When *Fast & Furious* came out in 2009, the movie made more than $360 million worldwide. Both the seventh and eighth installments have made more than $1 billion. Some critics have said the movies are just out to make a lot of money, but others have warmed to the films. Critics have given high ratings to the most recent films.

The filmmakers surpass themselves with each new release. They wow audiences with more outlandish action and take cars to places no one would expect. Cars crash through windows from one skyscraper to the next. They race across frozen ice, chased by a nuclear submarine. Cars even parachute from the sky.

And at least two more films are in the works. Diesel has signed on to play Dominic Toretto in upcoming films planned for release in 2019 and 2021.

Work-Life Balance

In the midst of filming *Fast & Furious*, Gadot became engaged to Israeli businessman Yaron Varsano. The couple married on September 28, 2008. Because of their commitments in Israel and the United States, the couple traveled back and forth a lot. They stayed in hotels almost constantly. But they soon discovered that some hotels also have apartments. The couple was eager to rent one. With all their travel, it was important to them to have a place that felt like home.

This experience inspired the couple, along with Varsano's brother, to open their own luxury five-star hotel in Tel Aviv, Israel, called The Varsano Hotel. The hotel includes spacious apartments that are modern and cozy. Guests appreciate the quiet privacy as well as the views of the nearby Mediterranean Sea. Gadot and her husband worked together to make the hotel a success. Gadot even spent time changing the sheets when they were getting the business up and running.

Gadot continued to travel back and forth between Israel and the United States for auditions and acting jobs. She filmed an episode of the TV series *Entourage* in 2009. In 2010 she appeared in the movie *Date Night*, which starred Steve Carell and Tina Fey. And when filming began for the next Fast and the Furious film, Gadot was called on board.

In *Fast Five*, Gadot played Yashar again. She was very excited to revisit this character. Gadot said, "Most of the

Gadot sits on a motorcycle on the set of *Fast Five.*

female characters you see in films today are 'the poor heartbroken girl.' That's why I'm so proud of the *Fast* movies. I feel like Gisele is an empowering woman."

The new role used Gadot's military knowledge. In the film, Toretto calls Yashar in as a weapons specialist to help with a heist. Gadot also got an opportunity to ride a motorcycle. The Ducati motorcycle they put her on for the film was larger than what she was used to, so Gadot learned from the experts how to manage the bike.

Fast Five was released in 2011. That same year, Gadot gave birth to her first child, Alma. She said that becoming a mother was hugely rewarding, but Gadot had to face the challenges of having a young child while pursuing an international acting career. Gadot sometimes felt guilty about taking her young daughter on airplanes to different countries. But she also knew she was showing her daughter that it is important to work hard and to pursue the job she loves.

In the first two years after Alma was born, Gadot landed some acting roles in Israel. She starred as Kika on the TV series *Asfur*. The following year she got a role in another Israeli series called *Kathmandu*.

In 2013 Gadot returned again to the Fast and the Furious family. In *Fast & Furious 6*, Yashar has been dating Han Seoul-Oh, a racer who made his debut in *Tokyo Drift*. The two are recruited to help stop a team of drivers who are trying to steal a top-secret weapon. In her final scene, Yashar is hanging off the edge of a moving car. When she sees one of their rivals coming up behind them, she lets go. She sacrifices herself so she

Gadot works on an intense scene in *Fast & Furious 6*.

Gadot's husband, Yaron Varsano

can shoot their rival and save Seoul-Oh. Fans were forced to say goodbye to this beloved character.

In 2015 Gadot's husband and his brother made a major deal. A Russian billionaire named Roman Abramovich was interested in the hotel in Tel Aviv. He wanted to convert it into a home for himself, so the Varsanos sold the property.

Meanwhile, Gadot was struggling to find new acting roles. Since her Fast and the Furious character had died, she could no longer rely on the films to keep her working. Gadot had been spending a lot of time traveling back and forth between Tel Aviv and Los Angeles. She auditioned for roles, but nothing was working out. She got plenty of callbacks. She did camera tests for the casting directors. But in the end, they all came back to say someone else had gotten the role. Gadot considered giving up acting.

Then her agent called with yet another audition. It was a secret role. Gadot wasn't allowed to know anything about it yet. Not knowing what she was walking into, Gadot hopped a flight to Los Angeles.

Wonder Woman for a New Age

Zack Snyder, a movie director famous for making movies based on comic book stories, was waiting to meet with Gadot. He was pleased to see the actor and have her read lines. But even then, he could not tell her what role he was casting. Gadot knew that Snyder was working on a new Batman movie, so she thought she might be auditioning for a role as Catwoman.

When she was called back to do a camera test, Gadot still didn't know what the part was or what movie it was for. Snyder tentatively asked her if Wonder Woman was well known in Israel. She was. Gadot had heard of Wonder Woman, but she didn't know much about her or her story. Even so, Gadot was thrilled about the role. She explained, "Anytime I had general meetings in LA, I always said that my dream role was to do an empowered, independent woman who doesn't rely on men."

But Gadot didn't have the role yet. As part of the audition, she still had to do a screen test with actor Ben Affleck, who would also be in the new film. Several other actors were also auditioning for the Wonder Woman role.

Gadot performs a scene with Affleck.

Gadot was nervous as she waited for her chance to do the screen test. She and the other actors had to stay in their own trailers until they were called in for their turn. Gadot called her husband, who suggested she get pumped up in her trailer by listening to Beyoncé's music. Gadot blasted the music and danced to calm her nerves. She says Beyoncé made her feel empowered before the big audition.

The audition went well, and Gadot and Affleck worked well together on-screen. Still, it took another six weeks before Gadot heard back about the role. By then she assumed that someone else had gotten the part, so she was shocked when she turned her phone on after a flight to see twenty missed calls from her agent. She had gotten the role!

Gadot was elated. She had beaten at least six other actors who were up for the part, including Olga Kurylenko, who played the role in *Quantum of Solace* that Gadot had auditioned for at the beginning of her acting career. Gadot was also nervous. This was a big role. And it was still a secret, so she couldn't tell anyone about it.

Gadot's Wonder Woman would make her first appearance in the DC Comics film *Batman v Superman: Dawn of Justice.* The movie was released in March 2016. It starred Affleck as Batman and Henry Cavill as Superman. The two heroes are at odds. Batman doesn't

Left to right: Affleck, Gadot, and Henry Cavill pose together as Batman, Wonder Woman, and Superman.

know if he should allow Superman to fight humanity's battles. Superman, on the other hand, doesn't think Batman should be able to take law and order into his own hands. When Batman and Superman eventually team up to defeat a Doomsday monster that the villain Lex Luthor has unleashed, Wonder Woman also joins the fight. She flies through the air, attacking the monster with her sword. She manages to cut off the beast's hand before Superman ultimately takes the monster down.

Overall, *Batman v Superman* received negative reviews. Viewers thought there were too many special effects. Many said that director Zack Snyder failed to bring out the best aspects of these popular and beloved characters. However, many critics thought Gadot as Wonder Woman was the best part of the film. Gadot's performance left movie fans excited to see Wonder Woman in her own film.

They did not have to wait long. *Wonder Woman* was already in the

Gadot poses as Wonder Woman.

Jenkins gives Gadot direction on the set of *Wonder Woman.*

making. Director Patty Jenkins was hired in April 2015 to begin work on the project. And there was a lot of pressure to make this film a success. This would be the first big-budget, female-led superhero movie in more than a decade and the first ever directed by a woman. Many fans had high hopes for the movie, and Jenkins and Gadot felt pressure to give fans a movie they would love. They also hoped that the movie might open more opportunities for women to work on big-budget Hollywood films.

Gadot also wanted to make a movie that would teach her daughter something. Gadot wants more strong stories about women to be made. But during filming, she tried not to think about the pressure. She wanted to make sure she was presenting the character of Wonder Woman in the best way she could.

Gadot went through six months of physical training to prepare for the part of Wonder Woman. She said her workouts were more intense than anything she had experienced before—including boot camp in the Israeli army. She practiced kung fu, kickboxing, sword fighting, jujutsu, and horseback riding. The slender Gadot got into fighting shape. Through her training, she gained seventeen pounds—all muscle.

Gadot acted opposite Chris Pine, who played Steve Trevor, an English soldier spying on the German army. Diana joins him, hoping that she can put an end to all war. Having grown up on a protected island, Diana knows nothing of the ways of the world. But she is determined to use her power to bring about change.

Jenkins directs a scene with Gadot and Chris Pine (*right*) for *Wonder Woman*.

Wonder Baby

While *Wonder Woman* was still in production, Gadot became pregnant with her second child. When it came time to do reshoots on certain scenes, Gadot was five months pregnant. To accommodate her changing body, costume designers had to cover her pregnant belly with a green cloth. That way, they could digitally alter the scenes later so she looked as she did in the rest of the film. Gadot gave birth to her daughter Maya in March 2017.

Gadot portrays Diana with a sense of innocence that makes audiences root for her. Diana believes that humans are essentially good, and she wants to protect them from the horrors of war.

Audiences loved *Wonder Woman*. People filled the theaters, and critics wrote rave reviews of the film. The story was interesting, and Wonder Woman was smart, graceful, and confident. In many superhero films, critics say fight scenes are too dramatic or happen too frequently. But Wonder Woman's fights were subtler, and she used her powers to protect and defend. Many critics and fans believed that *Wonder Woman* lived up to the hype. It was an inspiring film that showed girls they could be more than just a side character in the story. Girls and women could be superheroes, and girls and women would attend superhero movies.

Gadot was a Wonder Woman for the modern generation. Parents had an opportunity to take their daughters to a film that shows a strong, female role model. "For girls, it was always the princess being saved. Now we have Wonder Woman—she's fearless, proactive, she believes in herself and she believes she can do everything. That's a true woman for me," said Gadot.

Just a few short years after Gal Gadot had considered quitting acting, she took on a major role as an inspiring superhero. With more Wonder Woman films on the horizon, Gadot intends to continue to inspire the next generation of girls to become a new kind of princess.

Important Dates

1985   Gal Gadot is born on April 30, in Rosh HaAyin, Israel.

2004   She wins the Miss Israel pageant and represents her country in the Miss Universe pageant.

2005   She begins her two-year service in the Israeli Defense Forces.

2006   She serves in the IDF during the Israel-Hezbollah War in Lebanon and northern Israel.

2007   She studies law and international relations at IDC Herzliya but drops out to pursue an acting career.
        She lands her first acting role on the Israeli TV show *Bubot*.

2008   She marries businessman Yaron Varsano.

2009   She makes her first appearance as Gisele Yashar in *Fast & Furious*.

2011	She plays Yashar in *Fast Five*. Her daughter, Alma Varsano, is born.
2012	She appears in the Israeli TV show *Kathmandu*.
2013	She plays Yashar in *Fast & Furious 6*.
2015	Gadot and the Varsanos sell their hotel in Tel Aviv.
2016	She makes her debut as Wonder Woman in *Batman v Superman: Dawn of Justice*.
2017	She gives birth to her second child, Maya Varsano. *Wonder Woman* is released.

SOURCE NOTES

8   Elizabeth Wagmeister, "'Wonder Woman' Gal Gadot on Playing Lead Female Superhero: 'Growing Up, I Had Superman and Batman,'" *Variety*, May 26, 2017, http://variety.com/2017 /film/news/gal-gadot-wonder-woman-female-empowerment -superhero-1202446146/.

10 Sonaiya Kelley, "At 'Wonder Woman' Premiere, Forget Girl Power. It's about Gender Equality," *Los Angeles Times*, May 26, 2017, http://www.latimes.com/entertainment/movies/la-et-mn -wonder-woman-premiere-20170525-story.html.

12 Shiryn Ghermezian, "Living in Los Angeles, Actress Gal Gadot Says She Misses Israeli 'Chutzpah,'" *Algemeiner*, May 8, 2017, https://www.algemeiner.com/2017/05/08/living-in-los-angeles -actress-gal-gadot-says-she-misses-israeli-chutzpah/.

13 Marla Horn Lazarus, "Get Ready to Experience the Wonder of Gal Gadot," *Think Magazine*, June 1, 2017, http:// thinkmagazines.com/stars/get-ready-to-experience-the-wonder -of-gal-gadot/.

13 Laura Jacobs, "Meet Gal Gadot, Our New Wonder Woman," *Vanity Fair*, August 2015, http://www.vanityfair.com /hollywood/2015/07/gal-galdot-wonder-woman-miss-israel.

16 Samantha Schnurr, "Gal Gadot Is Just as Tough as Wonder Woman: 'Let's Own Who We Are and Use It as a Strength,'" *E Online*, July 3, 2016, http://www.eonline.com/fr/news/745815 /gal-gadot-is-just-as-tough-as-wonder-woman-let-s-own-who -we-are-and-use-it-as-a-strength.

18 Brendan Morrow, "Gal Gadot's Military Service: 5 Fast Facts You Need to Know," *Heavy*, last modified June 5, 2017, http://heavy .com/entertainment/2017/06/gal-gadot-military-service-israel -defense-forces/.

19 Ibid.

21 Lynn Hirschberg, "Gal Gadot Listened to Beyoncé to Prepare for Her Wonder Woman Audition," *W*, April 12, 2017, https://www .wmagazine.com/story/gal-gadot-wonder-woman-beyonce.

21 Marlow Stern, "Gal Gadot's Wonder Woman: A Hamas-Bashing, Ex-IDF Soldier and Former Miss Israel," *Daily Beast*, July 29, 2014, http://www.thedailybeast.com/gal-gadots-wonder-woman -a-hamas-bashing-ex-idf-soldier-and-former-miss-israel.

26 Michael d'Estries, "Gal Gadot's Rise from Law Student to Supermodel to Movie Star," *From the Grapevine*, June 9, 2017, https://www.fromthegrapevine.com/slideshows/arts/gal-gadot -movies-wonder-woman-batman-vs-superman-israeli-actress -model/page/3\.

26 Claire Hodgson, "10 Things You NEED to Know about Gal Gadot," *Cosmopolitan*, August 19, 2015, http://www .cosmopolitan.com/uk/entertainment/news/a37818/gal-gadot -wonder-woman-facts/.

30 Ibid.

33 John Nugent, "Exclusive: Gal Gadot Talks Wonder Woman's Role in *Batman v Superman*," *Empire*, last modified June 28, 2016, http://www.empireonline.com/movies/batman-v-superman -dawn-justice/batman-v-superman-wonder-woman-gal-gadot/.

40 Jennifer Read-Dominguez, "Gal Gadot Says Wonder Woman Is a REAL Role Model for Young Girls—Unlike Princesses," *Digital Spy*, June 8, 2017, http://www.digitalspy.com/movies/wonder -woman/news/a830223/gal-gadot-born-to-play-wonder-woman/.

SELECTED BIBLIOGRAPHY

d'Estries, Michael. "Gal Gadot's Rise from Law Student to Supermodel to Movie Star." *From the Grapevine*, June 9, 2017. https://www .fromthegrapevine.com/slideshows/arts/gal-gadot-movies-wonder -woman-batman-vs-superman-israeli-actress-model/page/3\.

"Gal Gadot." *Biography*. Last modified March 28, 2016. https://www .biography.com/people/gal-gadot-032916.

Ghermezian, Shiryn. "Living in Los Angeles, Actress Gal Gadot Says She Misses Israeli 'Chutzpah.'" *Algemeiner*, May 8, 2017. https://www .algemeiner.com/2017/05/08/living-in-los-angeles-actress-gal-gadot -says-she-misses-israeli-chutzpah/.

Hirschberg, Lynn. "Gal Gadot Listened to Beyoncé to Prepare for Her Wonder Woman Audition." *W*, April 12, 2017. https://www .wmagazine.com/story/gal-gadot-wonder-woman-beyonce.

Hodgson, Claire. "10 Things You NEED to Know about Gal Gadot." *Cosmopolitan*, August 19, 2015. http://www.cosmopolitan.com/uk /entertainment/news/a37818/gal-gadot-wonder-woman-facts/.

Jacobs, Laura. "Meet Gal Gadot, Our New Wonder Woman." *Vanity Fair*, August 2015. http://www.vanityfair.com/hollywood/2015/07/gal -galdot-wonder-woman-miss-israel.

Morrow, Brendan. "Gal Gadot's Military Service: 5 Fast Facts You Need to Know." *Heavy*. Last modified June 5, 2017. http://heavy.com /entertainment/2017/06/gal-gadot-military-service-israel-defense -forces/.

Nugent, John. "Exclusive: Gal Gadot Talks Wonder Woman's Role in *Batman v Superman*." *Empire*. Last modified June 28, 2016. http:// www.empireonline.com/movies/batman-v-superman-dawn-justice /batman-v-superman-wonder-woman-gal-gadot/.

Schnurr, Samantha. "Gal Gadot Is Just as Tough as Wonder Woman: 'Let's Own Who We Are and Use It as a Strength.'" *E! Online*, July 3, 2016. http://www.eonline.com/fr/news/745815/gal-gadot-is-just-as -tough-as-wonder-woman-let-s-own-who-we-are-and-use-it-as-a -strength.

Stern, Marlow. "Gal Gadot's Wonder Woman: A Hamas-Bashing, Ex-IDF Soldier and Former Miss Israel." *Daily Beast*, July 29, 2014. http:// www.thedailybeast.com/gal-gadots-wonder-woman-a-hamas -bashing-ex-idf-soldier-and-former-miss-israel.

FURTHER READING

BOOKS

Landau, Elaine. *Beyoncé: R & B Superstar.* Minneapolis: Lerner Publications, 2013. Read this book to learn more about the popular artist who inspired Gadot as well as countless other women and girls through her fun and empowering music.

Rucka, Greg. *The Lies.* Burbank, CA: DC Comics, 2017. Check out this Wonder Woman comic to learn more about the story of Diana as she unearths the secrets of her past.

Schatz, Kate. *Rad American Women A–Z.* San Francisco: City Lights, 2015. Take a look at these short biographies of diverse female artists, abolitionists, scientists, and more who have created important change in American history.

WEBSITES

DC Comics: Wonder Woman
http://www.dccomics.com/characters/wonder-woman
Learn more about Wonder Woman, including her history, superpowers, and where you can see her in comic books and other media.

Gal Gadot
http://www.galgadot.com
Check out Gadot's official website to learn more about her life and current work.

Smithsonian: The Surprising Origin Story of Wonder Woman
http://www.smithsonianmag.com/arts-culture/origin-story-wonder-woman-180952710/
Read this article to learn more about the creation of Wonder Woman.

INDEX